# Little River

*poems by*

# Paul Stroble

*Finishing Line Press*
Georgetown, Kentucky

# Little River

*For Beth and Emily*

Copyright © 2017 by Paul Stroble
ISBN 978-1-63534-136-2 First Edition
All rights reserved under International and Pan-American Copyright Conventions.
No part of this book may be reproduced in any manner whatsoever without written permission from the publisher, except in the case of brief quotations embodied in critical articles and reviews.

ACKNOWLEDGMENTS

"Channel Cat," "Giving Away His Clothes," and "Stereoscope" appeared in *Pegasus*. My thanks to editor Becky Lindsay. "Stereoscope" won first place in the Kentucky State Poetry Society's 2016 Adult Contest.

"The Genealogist" appeared in *Springhouse*. My thanks to editor Brian DeNeal.

"Little River" appeared in *Big Muddy* in a slightly different form. My thanks to editor Dr. Susan Swartwout.

"Pumpjacks." The final lines allude to Thoreau's *Walden*, the chapter "Where I Live, and What I Lived For": "I have frequently seen a poet withdraw, having enjoyed the most valuable part of a farm, while the crusty farmer supposed that he had got a few wild apples only. Why, the owner does not know it for many years when a poet has put his farm in rhyme, the most admirable kind of invisible fence, has fairly impounded it, milked it, skimmed it, and got all the cream, and left the farmer only the skimmed milk."

"Chautauqua" was inspired by the account in Lewis Atherton, *Main Street on the Middle Border* (1954, 1984).

Many thanks to Dwight Bitikofer, Heather Derr-Smith, Mary Biddinger, David Clewell, David Greenhaw, Jane Ellen Ibur, Stacey Stachowicz, the Novel Neighbor bookstore, the Webster Groves Starbucks, and especially my friend and mentor Tom Dukes. Thanks also to Steven L. Grigg, whose book *Reflections: The Nickel Plate Years, Clover Leaf District* inspired the railroad poems and provided facts in "Railroad Man"; and to classmates Kathy Schultz and Sherry Smith-Stanford, whose genealogical work inspired "The Genealogist." Many thanks to Leah Maines and everyone at FLP.

Publisher: Leah Maines
Editor: Christen Kincaid
Cover Art: Paul Stroble
Author Photo: Beth Stroble
Cover Design: Elizabeth Maines

Printed in the USA on acid-free paper.
Order online: www.finishinglinepress.com
　　　　　also available on amazon.com

Author inquiries and mail orders:
Finishing Line Press
P. O. Box 1626
Georgetown, Kentucky 40324
U. S. A.

# Table of Contents

### I
Testimony ........................................................................... 1
Channel Cat ....................................................................... 2
Pumpjacks ......................................................................... 3
Locusts .............................................................................. 4
Fossils ............................................................................... 5
Traveling Man .................................................................. 6
County Seat ...................................................................... 7

### II
Wender's Crossing .......................................................... 10
1910 Postcard ................................................................. 11
Stereoscope ..................................................................... 12
Young Death ................................................................... 13
Chautauqua .................................................................... 14
Northeast of Marytown ................................................. 15
Railroad Man ................................................................. 16
*En Plein Air* ................................................................... 17
Ephraim .......................................................................... 18
Rock City Barn .............................................................. 19
The Genealogist ............................................................. 20
Giving Away His Clothes .............................................. 21

### III
Motel Matchbook ........................................................... 24
Tea ................................................................................... 25
Little River ...................................................................... 26
"State Prison: Do Not Pick Up Hitchhikers" ................ 27
Glen Heck's Junk Yard .................................................. 28
Zion's Church Road ...................................................... 29
Scattering ........................................................................ 30
Fireflies ........................................................................... 31

I

**Testimony**

Blue fescue and Queen Anne's lace,
tarred poles grow by the highway
across river bottoms,
once rough forest roads
for my mothers and fathers.

I remember the white cross,
*Get Right with God,*
that stood along the road by the timber
swept by high water in '63,
to float upon Little River
to warn fishermen for their souls.

In old Marytown,
Beulah Church is a granary,
the auger at the broken-out window fulfills the Word,
*Bring the full tithe into the storehouse
so that there may be food in my house.*

Down the green ridge,
I say Amen to the claw-foot tub,
a trough for the cattle beneath the willow tree
that shades a junky half-acre,
a hawk perched on the rim,
living rust red against green.

I place my hand upon my heart,
and sing the hymns among the railroad tracks
and hear the catbirds
and the robins among the honeysuckle.
I walk down the aisle, and to my left
timber leans toward the sky from the slope
and to my right, James Creek,
high from summer rains, winds as a child's scrawl.

And at day's end I hear doves that remind me
of the dove that first taught me *melancholy*,
and I watch fireflies as Little River flows toward the Okaw

as I have so many times. Staying away is a fast
that cannot be long unbroken.

**Channel Cat**

Beneath the church road bridge,
at night on the river,
he listens to baseball:

*a solo blast with two outs
in the seventh and a two-run shot
in the eighth.*

He was baptized right here.
The water near carried away
both him and the preacher,
who caught a bluegill in his robe.

What a wonder the game doesn't
spook the fish,
and he's so happy
he forgets to check his trotlines,

but catfish can't swim by
without being tempted
on a starry night with good
moonlight, *a solo homer*

*off Browder in the ninth.*
just as he brings in
a real beauty,
good eating for Friday.

**Pumpjacks**

along the state road
by the timber

of family neighbors,
thirty liters of oil

a stroke from
sandstone pools

of Pennsylvanian
age along anticlines

of the Illinois Basin
throughout the county,

but not for us:
1940 test wells

on Grandpa's land
produced nothing,

unintended consequence
of land claims five

generations ago,
rich soil and timber beauty,

good fortune
thus far for family

plowing, harvesting,
trading in town

and for me, as Thoreau
would say, beloved lands

wandered, explored
and tapped for words

while the oil man
thinks he's the richer man.

**Locusts**

Twilight, the evening's manic,
red-eyed song in neighborhood trees,
hollow abdomens intensifying the flexing tymbals,
imagoes in bark, calling for mates.

To be odd and avoided,
to be odd and alluring,
like a stranger in a song.

We listened to locusts in their time,
summer nights by the corn
toward Zion's Church. We looked at one another,
        her direct gaze,
dark hair, doubled necklace of silver and moss agate.

The setting sun on the water tower,
the blue pasture beneath, that little house
of her uncle's that was on the market forever
because he wasn't serious about selling,
        yet he buried a St. Joseph's for blessing.

*Put me to the test, says the Lord,*

and the Lord opens blessings
through the windows of Heaven, the end of the locust,
produce abundant,
rich corn high enough
to block my view of the timber
and the old Clovis place.

Driving along the plowed fields,
I remember the way
Sandys painted Medea as a gypsy
making incantation over difficult ingredients.

She might as well have had locusts,
hollow dead on the plate,
their song remembered for summer nights.

**Fossils**

Sunday afternoon, our heads bowed
to the limestone

along the upper banks of Little River
where hunters like us

could be lucky and spot
brachiopods, cephalopods, ferns,

undergrowth sphenophyllum
in ironstone modules,

Paleozoic rock,
Mesozoic sediment,

perhaps even a trilobite,
my hope, if only a point

of its armor: sacred creatures
of diverse kinds in warm seas,

hardy for 300 million years
while on land only microbial

soil crust before the Permian
event, a treasure

for these far distant collectors…
like one I imagine epochs

from now, who scans a river's edge
and reaches for a rock,

point of a Holocene bone,
me in the limestone leaves.

**Traveling Man**

*This train is bound for glory*
that great old song,
and light rain falls
over the church road
at the IC tracks.

I'm home, no need to jump a train
or long for what I don't have
except as young dreams:

a traveling man,
seeking that clandestine marker
along the roadside,
a hospitable farm house
and hot stew ready…

an engineer of fame,
true to any schedule, with love
for every curve and field
and you set your watch
to my arrival…

a steampunk genius
with a train of my own,
freelance law enforcement
toward Cairo or Memphis,
St. Louis or Cleveland…

or a graffitist, tag PES,
bombing boxcars
with three-color throwups
that stop traffic
in every little Midwest town,

undaunted and legendary.

**County Seat**

Bicycle tires,
small town birds
singing in neighbors' trees,
a car beep in the distance.

Riding, the boy sees the way
the sidewalks have raised
as neighbors' trees grew beneath
and pushed upward,

and as he pauses from his hot ride
through undulating streets
he likes the coleus and moss rose
that line the walk of 263 Sixth.

Beneath the phone poles,
lined in matched order down Washington Street,
the oak and maple are still
full green shade.

He pedals to the outskirts
where the expired line crosses
St. Louis Street, and he stands in blue
to gaze down the bright right of way.

At the cemetery, folks
have already decorated: kin needful
of flowers, flags. His grandparents
at the lane's turn have forget-me-nots.

He remembered this as a bored day,
no one around, nothing to do,
when his home became for him always
as the shadow of God's wings.

II

## Wender's Crossing

Should he swim?
The ferry isn't running,
but he needs to get into town
to fetch the horse
        at Johnston's livery.

The trees are all gold and brown,
like the *Eschen* he loved as a boy
and held onto a branch with one hand
for the longest time.

He thinks of Bremen,
the three-month passage
on the galliote *Fortuna*,
the friends he made, who scattered
        upon arrival at New Orleans,
the writing on the manifest.

Everything is caught up,
debts paid in full.
When winter follows autumn
        the snow piles up
and the ferry seldom runs
        for the ice froes.
He watches the geese. He laughs,

a free man among a free people,
a fiddle-player who fiddles
a fair Mozart, a better square dance.
He thinks of his wife and young son,
        who born here could be president.
Should he swim?

**1910 Postcard**

Men in hats and suits smoke cigars beside the door
of the Albright Hotel. The streets look like dirt.
      There are horses.
A wagon retreats down the street
beside facades of iron. See there?
At the block's end, one car in town.

That's likely Walter McElroy.
In Nineteen-nine
      he sold his partnership
and bought an Everitt 30. He drives up one street
and down the next
and sometimes he drives all the way to Springfield
so he can visit Lincoln's home.

Upper stories of businesses, drapery,
within, leading families' bachelor sons
whose habits are disapproved, discussed,
never punished, finally erased
like telephone lines on postcards.

With your magnifying glass
you read signs above the men, the National Bank,
Spring's Furniture and Coffins,
Dowie Hotel, with the sky, facades and dirt,
      hand-colored, rural values.

Are the women forbidden in this agora?
They're on the reverse,
sitting in parlors, in silk grosgrain and crochet lace.
They write in cursive, sweet messages
to family in other towns
then moisten one-cent stamps.

**Stereoscope**

Aunt Friede got eye strain,
the viewer pressed against her face
so often, each image to each eye
and then blending,
that addictive
illusion of depth and dimension.

It's not that she didn't love the farm,
plowed by her own father
who died on the front forty,
nor did she long for more of the world
than what she'd seen
and what would have saved to see.

But she fancied traveling the globe
as a stereographer, visiting place after place
from Washington
to the Taj Mahal to the Cliffs of Moher

and any place worthy
of a dream's double image.

**Young Death**

My mother's cousin died
eating too many berries.
She was young,
and was buried along the banks of the river.
She had forgotten where.
        Who knows by now,
how the water may have washed away
whatever stone marked her place, washed her grave?

It was a big family: fifteen children,
six grew past infancy,
and two died in meager adolescence,
of dropsy and of berries.

*Did families grieve back then?* asked a student,
*or were they so used to death that they moved on.*
*I couldn't stand to lose a child!*
I thought of Mary Lincoln,
unable to leave her bedroom
for a year after the death of Willie,
and broken Abraham needful to be strong
for both and the nation.

I watched the river from a distance,
fearful of its speed,
a tributary with tree limbs
and fishermen's cups toward the great channel
first seen by Marquette
who, fearful of being forgotten, asked
that his grave be marked with a cross.

**Chautauqua**

Bright Sunday afternoon, the still-kept field
at our own Chautauqua Lake
where we walk,

dream of that eager event for the better people,
weeks of anticipation, parents shamed
into taking their children
for uplift and education.

Up went the shelter tents of God's wings,
where children kick manna corn cobs
toward Heaven, speakers dipped hands
into ice water because of the heat
inside the blessed canopies.

*Come home, sinner, come home…*
*The secrets of character…*
*The Slavic church in America….*
*The faith of Abraham Lincoln…*

Beautiful days, beautiful times,
our town assembled beneath these trees
that even then were tall along the grass and water.

*What killed the beautiful days?*
the *Gazette* editor mourned, but no days last.
We became busy,
        going down to the Gem Theatre
for double features, hot popcorn,
Tom Pilcher the piano player
kept the suspense going. More movies,
and summer circuits never returned.

She told me her grandparents
kissed through *Lucille Love, Girl of Mystery,*
while back at the lake,
William Jennings Bryan preached,

and that was the theatre where they saw
dear brother Fred in the newsreel of troops,
before he went missing on Okinawa.

**Northeast of Marytown**

Old growth maple and pin oak
against the washed out field,
the ribs of a horse,
unearthed from last summer's rain.
Now, the earth is hard.
A goldfinch lights upon the blossom
of meadow foxtail, mourning dove,
always heard, invisible, gray against gray.

When you don't know how far,
the walking seems endless,
but on the fields beside the woods,
you want time to stretch,
a companionable hike adapted
to the sun's slow arc.

We ate blackberries from the vine,
the vine around the truck of the willow
that grew with the blue spruce.
We saw sand hill cranes, black-necked stilts.
*Damn beavers*, he said, without humor
toward the mound of branches,
trench between the ridges
of glacial origin through this river valley.

The *Dao De Jing:* nothing is more
yielding than water, but for moving
the strong, nothing is better,
including ice, pushing the valleys,
depositing till, creating topography,
and indirectly, souls.

At last, beneath a willow tree and blue spruce
growing beside one another,
the white tombstone marks
the place of the body, gone the way of earth,
the first white settler of this county,

just a boy when he began a life
honored in the local histories, "so long ago,"
saw five wild turkeys run into the woods

and, there, built a lean-to against a maple
on the ridge, began to turn the loam for a field,
set out with his rifle day after day.

## Railroad Man

On the front porch by the tracks,
Charlie Bruner talks and talks about trains.
*Here is a 4-6-0 passenger locomotive,*
*built in 1900 in Virginia. A beauty!*

He lives past the junction tower,
where in the morning fog
water tank pedestals past the coal deck
come in and out beyond Hodstown's Third Street.

Hike back six dozen years,
and there was a newspaper in town
called *The Age of Steam and Fire*,
his dad's own age, when he worked
the Illinois Central, all over:
Centralia, up to Bloomington,
on the eastward prairie
and down to Cairo and the rivers.

*This is a 2-8-2 Mikado,*
*common on the Nickel Plate Line*
*west of Frankfort, and here*
*the Nickel Plate met the IC.*

Towns spring up along tracks
where there had not even been a wagon road,
not even a house the year before.
He saw the conversion of locomotives
from cord-wood to Illinois coal,
so many ton-miles of freight, by the time
he bought out that hotel in Magenville.

*Here is a 1000 series caboose.*
*We saved that one from scrap*
*and set it up at Marytown,*
*where it's Santa's House at Christmastime.*

Songbirds like chords on the power lines,
he lives to hear the clickety-clack of steel wheels
across rail joints, to watch the fireflies in their season.

*Life rushes toward the river,*
*but thanks be to God*
*the clatter and the fireflies slow it down.*

*En Plein Air*

Sunday afternoon homecoming
at the pond behind Beulah Church.
Monet forever reminds me of these lilies
and a day in the 1950s,
as if Monet's doppelgänger was Great-Grandpa Stew
gathering relatives at Giverny,
"painting as a bird sings."

By the haystacks behind the church,
I drank my soda, belched,
and hoped the adults could move it along.
        But Uncle Siebert called me back,
asked if he'd told me of the month
he ate only bits of his buddies' uniforms

washed down with piss and muddy water,
and the time he killed 217 Germans by himself
in spite of being shot 18 times,
twice in the head.
*I nearly died, believe you me,*
*but I recovered in the countryside.*

Brownie camera photos passed around.
Friede sighed, *I take a terrible picture.*
In this picture she sits with Charlie
who wears his overalls,
shows off the bushel basket of sienna gourds.
There is Granddad,
        born the year Bazille died,
out there in his field
beyond the place that smelled
of potatoes and mud daubers,
ten million cats mewing for sugar milk.

*I ain't lying when I tell you*
*you never saw such a beautiful thing*
*like a French sun on the haystacks,*
        laughed our impressionist,
and skipped a stone past the lilies.

## Ephraim

Drive toward Little River
on County Seat Road,
a path no longer known
west of Zion's Church where timber and dark soil

and durable water
assembled forty families
from one state and another
to the speculator's call,

though survivors became names
listed or missing from the census,

plains east to west, a hotel, stores,
cabins, a built-up road passage
in seasons with the breath of low water
to the north.

There were stones set down for memory
and even these are lost in bramble,
space left unplowed,
a bouquet of new growth oak,
history's flowers of the field

after the advance of desolate wilderness,
fevers, crops failed in two bad years
by the heavy hand of grief
that, still cruel, drew the railroad line
eight miles southeast.

The best land in many counties
waved with finest wheat,
and trees west and east
call the town Forsaken.

**Rock City Barn**

*To Miss Rock City Would Be a Pity*
on pitch black boards, fond ruin
and freehand letters form a ghost sign
on Granddad's barn, as the older ad
for Mail Pouch Tobacco shows through.

Down US 41 to 72 around
the Tennessee River,
Dad's fried chicken in foil,
unwashed skillets
left to sit upon our stovetop for two weeks.

Tearful Cherokee lands,
where rich families made summer retreat,
where clouds and smoke surrounded
hand to hand combat, blue and gray blood
in the heights of the Cumberland Plateau.

It was the soldiers who claimed
you could see seven states,
where now tourists wander observed
by gnomes, our land of the free.
Dad, bulky then, had trouble
at Fat Man's Squeeze
then always asked if I remembered that.

We paid and rode the train straight up,
to Mom's terror. In limestone,
those soluble caves, a once sealed off
carboniferous place: the famous waterfall
uncovered by the man whose wife's name
was Ruby, water colored with light.

Back down the mountain,
fried chicken long gone from our two-lane
sedan, a family restaurant at last.

It would've been a pity!
Cherish the barn while it stands,
live long, and watch the ghost signs
ask what we remember.

## The Genealogist

On a breezy day at the cemetery
her cap blew off.
She needed to find the stone
for Cyrene Wender.

She'll tell you
that the Wenders are shirt-tail cousins
by the young daughter
of great-great-grandmother Rachel McKay.
Her husband James remarried,
but went missing at the Battle of Columbus.

She followed her cap as it tumbled
among the graves,
and there was the stone,
where Cyrene has been since 1855.
A hawk flew over.
She walked, following it, looked down,
and found another grave she needed.

It's not usually so easy.
Census records:
        what happened to the wife,
the child listed in 1850 but not 1860?
A will is missing;
a name is misspelled and thus overlooked,
lives ephemeral as wind.
For years she has searched
        for James' father's name.

But now, the Wenders are accounted for
        in Beulah township.
Some sleep in an open place.
Some sleep in a place of timber,
        with God's shade in all weather.
They sleep in bytes: names and kin and dates.

**Giving Away His Clothes**

Here is the outfit he wore
for our church pictures,
and summer shirts I purchased
for him, but he hadn't yet worn

because, vague and stubborn,
he wore the same plaid polo
during his last three months.

Here are suits we pushed him into,
along with church during
his Christmas and Easter years.

By the time he got saved,
church clothes became casual,
so we didn't have to strain
top buttons for this very clip-on tie.

Today, these and all the rest---
good shoes, work slacks, shirts
in and out of style---go to charity.

He wore his Sunday best
for Eternity, where
clothes don't make the man.

III

**Motel Matchbook**

Wiping the dipstick clean with his fingers,
at the beginning of the S-curve
of U.S. 50 that never made any sense:

calm seasons of Americana, upswept
Googie design, hope for the future,
best pancakes at Dolly's,

diners who smile
for their own teenage songs
and put out their cigarettes in syrup.

The Parliament Motor Hotel beside:
starburst sign and egg blue cabins,
TV in every room, AC and heat;

two-digit phone, Lincoln
postcards, sodas in glass bottles
in the machine for a quarter.

Morning for the motel clerks
and the waitresses and all the drivers
of automobiles and pickups and big rigs.

Across the hay field,
a Union Pacific Streamliner
rushes passengers to St. Louis.

I want to stay,
but Dad says, *no, why would you stay
at a motel for a dollar fifty,*

*when we're only twenty miles from home?*
But he takes this matchbook
so he'll have some on hand.

To repeat time for simple days.

**Tea**

Sun tea grows brown in the noonday sun,
*Summer in the city,* I sing
while she lies in her hammock,
forgetful

    in our lazy days of summer,
the shed open to the life of the hard road
and the farm, laundry on the line
strung from trees that are hammock-ready.

    She's off today from Tri-City,
where she works the cash register.
Dad said, *I see Arlo at the store.*
*He comes to town to trade. Stan*
*sets out chairs for the old folks.*
*Arlo misses Sylvie so bad,* you say
*How are you?* and he cries a little.

    She's more brown each time
I come by. Her tea is going to be
too strong or spoiled.
But I can't tell you how much I forget:
car keys, chemistry homework,
somehow never song lyrics.

    *Wouldn't it be nice?* I sing.
She flips me off, but I think she likes me.
She offered me tea

but I had to get it myself and bring her one.
*Use Mom's purple tumblers,*
*not her Waterfordy glasses.*
I'd promise her new ones if I could.

Later, when I come home,
Dad says I'm sunburned, then sends me
to Tri-City and be sure to say hi to Arlo
if he's there, and squeeze his hand.

He sounds like a song,
*Your mother wants chamomile all the time,*
*but Lipton's fine for me.*

**Little River**

We had our sodas at the bait shop
at the end of the road down the hill,
a creek finally deep enough for a canoe.

I thought:
        Shiva pushed the glaciers
that pushed the channels
and from the god's hair, rushing water;

        Krishna held the chariot reins,
supreme manifestation of godhead,
teaching give no thought to gain or loss;

        Sarasvati, meandering, disappearing,
first mother and her blessed song,
road carrying life to heaven;

        The God of Israel,
whose prophet Amos calls up
the mighty river of justice,
whose chariots and throne are aflame,
Elisha calling, *My father, my father!*

From here I see beyond sycamore,
the Baptist steeple,
as it has been for two hundred years.

Countryside baptizes stories,
pioneer cabins in boundaries of timber,
flames of the prairie grass,
waters of justice, creek waters of memory.
They must flow together somewhere,
and the river water fills the stream.

Lord of the branches
rushing southwest, the streams float toward rivers,
unassuming access along banks
of sycamore
where we push off in the boat

and call upon the God we seek,
who raises up the hills
who draws channels of water with a Word.

## "State Prison: Do Not Pick Up Hitchhikers"

Cars and trucks on this highway, day and night,
but once, our railroad mattered more:
the Nickel Plate Line, Clover Leaf District,
drowning the words of God on Sundays
with the clatter and whistle.

On plats, it cut across the farms
        of Paul McKay, Sarah Wender,
Crescentia Harmon, August Strobel,
the highway but a faint trace on 1800s maps.

The old line was narrow gauge the year Grandpa was born.
Great-Grandpa helped put in the standard gauge line,
then Daddy and his brother worked on the route toward East St. Louis
and drank in the clubs
alongside the meatpackers off their shifts.

We lived where the right of way parallels Tower Street,
but the line is gone now.
Jog the right of way with your music and not fear
missing a whistle's warning, rain or shine.

The house is still there,
sunlight and white and empty for years,
brown at the high water mark.
Backyard tire ruts become the alley
along the backsides of all the houses.
Kids cut through toward the six blocks of Marytown
to get sodas at the store along the hard road.

In time, I will start here and walk
through Cowden, Ramsey, Sorento, Alhambra,
night and day, with sounds of night creatures in the brush,
rustling sounds in the brush,
all the way to the great channel,
and I'll hear the beat of the trains
        on the MacArthur bridge, like East St. Louis jazz.

## Glen Heck's Junk Yard

Twenty-acre field, crumpled metal
and blown rubber, prayers for safety,
prayers for solace. Nearby,
the pier goes out into the pond,
a child fishing with a grandfather or uncle,
backs to the wrecks.

Glen has the full text
of John 3:16 on his garage,
which you can see, and be reminded
as you drive this way.
He painted it himself and it's not very good,
but he did his best.

I lived just north, where my neighbor's field
was black with birds after harvest time.
I clapped my hands
just to see them rise,
to hear the call. Soon they were back.

That gave me hope,
the old story of bread on the water,
relinquishment of what will return.

Glen ponders when you walk the field together
for that certain auto part:
*Jesus could have done brain surgery like a pro.*
*He knew everything. He just didn't have the technology.*

*But he didn't need the technology,*
*as he created 10,000 meals*
*from the boy's bread and fish,*
*and healed blind eyes with spit.*

Beulah Township is not *ha'aretz*,
by any stretch, though Little River
is wide like the Jordan. Glen says, *here we read of the Land,*
*which is to say we read the Good Book here*
*and cast its words onto the places of our journeys,*
*solace and grief and blessing.*

At the pond by the wrecks, someone put up a 10-foot cross
to witness to passersby as Glen hopes for his sign.
*Christ's stone rolled away, like a semi truck tire.*

## Zion's Church Road

The sign grows hand-painted among cat-tails:
*Seven Miles to Zion's Church.*

These are gravel miles,
where saints live their family farms
and crop rows rush toward the timber.
I roll down the window,
accept dust upon good clothes
to hear the willful ignorance of the jays,
the doves' blues.

These circling dark birds:
death comes daily to timber,
and mourning has no part there,
though we say the willow weeps.

Above, clouds were what they are,
droplets around particles of dust,
billions in the cool upper air,
and contrails dash across.

A child thinks: *God shapes clouds,
the ice cream cone, the rabbit, and the leaf.*

We float with currents, we drift,
so we are dust. Are we clouds?
Something lodges our love
in the highest places
and another love reaches back.

Today, one cloud for me is the willow
        of Zion's Church
where we will bury him.
Another is a dove, another
is the praying hands of Dürer,
and another is the journey, sure
as all else changes, all seven miles.

**Scattering**

Sunday picnics on the river bank, fishing poles
propped by rocks, lovers with their music
        stroll the grassy lane.
No one would have been swimming
unless they now regretted life.
The river is small as they go
but cold, swift, with its own authority.
Parents hold children's hands at the water's edge.

1890. He didn't regret life, only
the spooked horse that upended
the wheat drill on the front forty
so that he fell hard into the lever,
        bled internally for a day,
a story no one wanted to tell
across decades

until we were ourselves there, in the field,
        in the bitter bedroom,
these boundaries of timber
that hid pioneer cabins, boundaries
for fields yearly tilled along
the state highways, livelihoods
for all the generations.

        I don't know where
I'd like to be buried, or where to be scattered,
perhaps samples of me
out the car window
down the church road,
starting at the river.

**Fireflies**

*The enzyme luciferase,*
*oxygen with luciferin and calcium*
*produce a cool, efficient light, but they only live*
*a few months, and return to the earth.*

Bobby also liked to explain
that Heaven is hotter than Hell.
*The melting point of brimstone, Rev. 21:8,*
*has a cooler melting point than seven times*
*the brightness of the sun, Isaiah 30:26.*
So when he said, *Go to Hell*
he was being positive,
but not everyone took it that way.

I said to him, *they're both hot, so let's call Heaven summer,*
*and fireflies are angels we can catch.*
That's the way with new doctrine,
innovators misunderstood, heretics
destroyed, then ideas take hold, develop.

We believed at Zion's Church in the Rapture.
He said, *You'd puke, so afraid of heights*
*You'd look down, puke, and God*
        *would let you go. Remember Lot's wife.*
I'd no answer. Just because it's the Rapture
doesn't mean I wouldn't get dizzy,
seeing the river recede as I climb.

But so much beyond our sight is merely terrestrial:
insect populations, radiation arcs,
the magnetism of the poles, strata beneath.
Reliably we reach toward things of earth
and things of Heaven.

I daydream at the river bank.
Questions have the aroma of summer,
seasons teach the dharma, the primordial sound.
        *God said, Let there be light,*
and he separated the waters.

I declare fireflies a new religious symbol
beside the eagle and the lion and the dove:
God's light, small for open hands.

**Paul Stroble** teaches philosophy and religious studies at Webster University in St. Louis and is also adjunct faculty at Eden Theological Seminary. Previously he taught at the University of Akron, Indiana University Southeast, Louisville Seminary, and Northern Arizona University. He is a native of Vandalia (Fayette County), Illinois. A grantee of the National Endowment for the Humanities and the Louisville Institute, he has written several books, primarily church related, and also numerous articles, essays, and curricular materials. He blogs at paulstroble.blogspot.com. His previous chapbook with Finishing Line Press, with the same fictional geography as this one, is *Dreaming at the Electric Hobo* (2015).

www.ingramcontent.com/pod-product-compliance
Lightning Source LLC
LaVergne TN
LVHW041602070426
835507LV00011B/1255